Cupid's Arrow

An international collection of love poetry

Creative Talents Unleashed

Anthologies Published by Creative Talents Unleashed

I Have a Name

Down The Rabbit Hole

Poetic Shadows – Ink and the Sword

Imperfect Paths

Shades of the Same Skin

Poetic Melodies

Divided Lines – A Poet's Stance

Writing Tips – Exploring the Writer's Path

Unleashed

Love, a Four Letter Word

GENERAL INFORMATION

Cupid's Arrow

By

Creative Talents Unleashed

1st Edition: 2018

This Publishing is protected under Copyright Law as a "Collection". All rights for all submissions are retained by the Individual Author and or Artist. No part of this publishing may be Reproduced, Transferred in any manner without the prior **WRITTEN CONSENT** of the "Material Owner" or its Representative Creative Talents Unleashed.

www.ctupublishinggroup.com

**Publisher Information
1st Edition: Creative Talents Unleashed
info@ctupublishinggroup.com**

This Collection is protected under U.S. and International Copyright laws

Copyright © 2018: Creative Talents Unleashed

ISBN-13: 978-1-945791-48-2 (Creative Talents Unleashed)
ISBN-10: 1-945791-48-9

Credits

Book Cover

Raja Williams

Book Description

Brenda-Lee Ranta

Creative Director

Mark Andrew Heathcote

Editors

Authors Responsible For Own Work

Introduction

Mark Andrew Heathcote

Introduction

The objective of this Anthology is to pay tribute to love and the concept of what we believe it to be.

Mark Andrew Heathcote, author of *In Perpetuity*

Contents

Introduction   v

Love at First Sight

Dancing Joy *Jackie Chou*	2
Anguish Soul *Christena AV Williams*	3
Fox Jewel Fire *Dah*	4
Tango *Jagari Mukherjee*	6
My Dearest *Christena AV Williams*	7
My Escape *Michelle Rice*	8
Love in a Local Train *Shyamal Mukhopadhyay*	9
Love at First Sight *Vincent Van Ross*	10
A Valentine's Day Poem *John Lambremont, Sr.*	11

Contents

Soul Catcher   12
Tammy S. Thomas

Love Everlasting

Half the World Apart   14
Gigi Lee

Wanting to Be With You   15
Jackie Chou

Eternal Love   16
Vincent Van Ross

Exhale   17
Paige Turner

Betel Leaves   18
Mark Andrew Heathcote

About Love   19
Hugh Burke

Fusion / Fission   20
Steven T. Licardi

A Lesson about Love   21
Lyne Beringer

Contents

Longing and Desire *James F. Cunningham*	22
Evermore *Valormore De Plume*	23
Where I Want to Be *Tammy S. Thomas*	24
Our Own Kind of Fairytale *Dena M. Daigle*	25
Written In the Stars *Elizabeth Esguerra Castillo*	26

Love of my Life

Intimate Moments *Raja Williams*	28
An Eternal Reward *William Wright, Jr.*	29
Paperback Writers *Lyne Beringer*	30
I Cannot Say You are Perfect *Estelle Powell*	31
Forgotten Places *Sue Lobo*	33

Contents

Be My Life   34
Sylvana Accom

The Soul of Eternal Love   35
Mark Andrew Heathcote

To: Two Doves   36
Christena AV Williams

A Bee to a Flower   37
Sravani singampalli

Closer View   38
Michele Rice

Three Stanzas for My Beloved   39
Jagari Mukherjee

I Remember   40
Liz Newman

Caressing Clichés into Comforting Sighs   43
Scott Thomas Outlar

Take Me Away   44
Maria Miraglia

Love Will Tear Us Apart

Missing   46
Mahinour Tawfik

Contents

Another Scar   47
Daginne Aignend

Bereft   49
Sanhita Baruah

Happiness in a Jar   50
Lyne Beringer

Rose Petals at My Feet   51
Mark Andrew Heathcote

Resonance of Love   52
Ken Allan Dronsfield

Cold Moon   53
Jagari Mukherjee

Saved by Words   54
Daginne Aignend

Tale of Woe   55
Mahinour Tawfik

The Bubble Bursts   56
Daginne Aignend

Love vs. Lust

Drifting With the Clouds   58
Jill N. Pontiere

Contents

Living in Loves Illusion   59
Raja Williams

I Am One With You   60
Sylvana Accom

Moonlight Away   61
Shola Balogun

Looks   62
Paige Turner

The Day I Wake To Find You   63
Gigi Lee

Perspiration   65
Sue Lobo

Summer, Ocean   66
Dah

The Goddess of Love   67
Audley Hitchins

The Millennials   68
Sagar Singh

Love is Forever

A Velvet Dawn   70
Ken Allan Dronsfield

Contents

Someday *Sanhita Baruah*	71
The Soul of My Life *Vincent Van Ross*	72
In the Delta *Sandra Lyon Kramer*	73
A Rare Luminosity *Heath Brougher*	75
First Kissed *John Walker*	76
Forever Love *Liz Newman*	77
Happy Mother's Day *John Lambremont, Sr*	78
Our Story *John Walker*	79
Anniversary *John Lambremont, Sr.*	80

Love Changes Everything

I.V. *Steven T. Licardi*	82

Contents

Lucky in Love *Jackie Chou*	84
Meeting *Lynn White*	85
My Stranger *Gigi Lee*	86
Baggage *Raja Williams*	88
Fall in Love *Sanhita Baruah*	89
Make Love to Me *Sue Lobo*	91
Petals *Linda Imbler*	92
Dormant *Steven T. Licard*	93
Dialect *Hugh Burke*	95
Convergence *Brenda-Lee Ranta*	96

Love Never Dies

Contents

A Letter to My Soulmate   98
Dena M. Daigle

Joie de Vivre   99
Paromita Mukherjee Ojha

Tinge of Tears in the Mist   100
Ken Allan Dronsfield

Blue   101
Lynn White

Heaven's Last Wish   103
Linda Imbler

Love   104
Mahinour Tawfik

Galveston   105
Linda Imbler

Thinking about Ex-boyfriend   106
Vatsala Radhakeesoon

Hold   108
Maggie Mae

Empty Pillow   109
Heath Brougher

Counting Stars   110
Sandra Lyon Kramer

Contents

Her Metaphor   111
Brenda-Lee Ranta

A Winter's Love (Later in Life)   112
Nolan P. Holloway, Jr.

Epilogue

The Starving Artist Fund   114

CTU Connections   116

About the Book   117

*Back Cover Poem Cupid's Arrow
Ajit Sripad Rao Nalkur

Love at First Sight

Dancing Joy

When you took my hand
for a waltz
I became
a butterfly
fluttering across the dance floor
with chiffon dress
and sparkly hair
drinking non-stop
the intoxicating air

I stare into your eyes
absorb your smile
your chest
a pillow for my head
your face
a flame in the night
under the revolving strobe light

Jackie Chou

Cupid's Arrow

Anguish Soul

Should our lips dine?
Paying the full bill
Indebted I will.

Should I fall so ailing?
That my soul burn in hell
Uncontrollable beyond blasphemy
Never have I anguish over a butterfly
As I do over you
It is sinful.

Branded for life
Unable to return to past lovers
The crack of ribcage
Churning of tripe
Nauseating of Insomnia
Should our lips dock?
It shall be my demise
Surely; only to satisfy my truth
As I am already fathom,
Adoring the nudity of your soul.

Christena AV Williams

Fox Jewel Fire

Winter's wet darkness
molds quickly
Along the town's edge
trees glitter
where night
loads its ravens

Autumn is left behind
like depleted love
A fox in silvery mist
is edgy,
its empty stomach's
hollow burn

On this night-path
in December's wound
I offer these words
You as lover, as jewel
a hovering fire
a fervid mouth

your hungry nails
along the breath
of my thighs
where you rose
to swill the juice
spilling over

and your eyes,

Cupid's Arrow

glistening chandeliers,
and me
a flamethrower
aimed at melting you
The white river, flowing

Dah

Tango

Bright flowers or translucent gems
That's what I wondered
When my eyes first met yours…
And I was surprised
At something so beautiful
That it went straight to my soul
Like a vintage record
And made me ache
With an unknown emotion
So that I could feel my breathing grow faster
As fantasies arose
On the stage of my imagination
With only you and I
Entangled in a never-ending tango…

Jagari Mukherjee

Cupid's Arrow

My Dearest

Is it not shame to call it love?
Love so endearing
Too forbidden
Must be fairy tale treasure Hunt; Monte Carlo
Do you pursue me like vultures?
Publicly tried me like Oscar Wilde
Is it not shame to call it love?
A tinker in my eye
A flinch in my touch
A faint spell when eyes meet
Is one so bewitched in despair even to whisper your name?
Stare at your blush
Is it not shame?
To call what may
Love!

Christena AV Williams

My Escape

My heart is complete and whole
You crept in and colored my soul
My love for you is glorious and new
My heart guides everything I do
But you've set the course to you
Now I'm stuck to you like glue
I've never felt like this before
From a romance novel, page is tore
Setting a plot, from dreams are made
Sign my name to your deed
Set your sails, our journey you lead
Escape in your heart, my only need
You store it very deep within
Your treasure chest you keep hidden
From anyone, who try to steal it
Inside of me, a fire you built
A flame that will burn eternally
For only you, my heart singularly
Beats to the same time as yours
You have dried up all my tears
From hidden pain, you've cured
You gifted your heart, I'm lured
To you, like fish to water
Now forever, dedicated to each other

Michelle Rice

Love in a Local Train

No, never traversed for thousand-of-years
        into dark alleys of Srawasti Vaishali
rather feel easy to commute for livelihood
           in local trains daily;
so many faces creating varied montage
        before my eyes visually
on a flash, a pair of deep kohled eyes
          pierced at me passingly
somewhere in obsession, the face stuck
          into mind unknowingly.

Boarding my local after a casual holiday,
a whisper" where had you been yesterday?"

Shyamal Mukhopadhyay

Cupid's Arrow

Love at First Sight

What started as a fleeting glance
Turned into a long, fixed stare
And, before he knew
What was happening
He had lost his heart

His very own heart
Refused to obey him
It popped out of his body
And, started circumambulating
The girl of its own choice

He wanted to shift his glance
And, look away from her
To avoid embarrassment
But, his eyes stayed right there
As if fixed by some superglue

His heart skipped several beats
Cold sweat broke out on his face
He fidgeted again and again
He fiddled with his fingers
The moment she stared back

He was doing so many things
That he had never done before
Just a fleeting glimpse of her
Is all it took for him to realise
That it was love at first sight

Vincent Van Ross

Cupid's Arrow

A Valentine's Day Poem

Angels sang the day we met:

Velvet voices filled my ear
As you swept by, so near and dear;
Loveliest maiden I'd seen yet,
Enticing eyes and a lively step;
Never knew exactly why
Time was then that I said "Hi;"
In the way, our race and tongue;
Never thought what we'd begun
Even now would keep us one,
Same as when we were so young.

Dearest one, you made me whole;
Always love me, heart and soul;
Years from now, when we've grown old,
Still you'll be the one I hold.

Please know this: for all my life,
Only you will be my wife;
Ever will our love bells ring,
Making those sweet angels sing.

John Lambremont, Sr.

Soul Catcher

You take my breath away
when my eyes capture your smile
Saving every moment we spend together
makes it worthwhile

I could dive into your spirit
and drown in your love
Revive me through your heart
and bless my soul
Truly the best love story ever told

You touch my very being
Loving you has taken a new height
The greatest destination of this flight

Tammy S. Thomas

Cupid's Arrow

Love Everlasting

Cupid's Arrow

Half the World Apart

I am in tomorrow
you are in yesterday
but here and now, we are together
it matters not, clock stops ticking

Moment knows no time
no respect for the sun
past goes on a blind date
with future dressed to the nines

Web is a bridge that defies quantum space
world apart, both on the same screen
native tongue, fourteen hours different
colors, in contrast, speaking the same language

We touch, not the skin but we mean
with keyboards, words that we penned
image clear, message dear, even not seen
a magic, cast by the net of singular feeling

Like a butterfly to a flower, kissing

Gigi Lee

Wanting to Be With You

If you are a disease
I shall seek no immunity
but cherish every symptom
every ounce of pain

If you are a defect
I shall be a flawed diamond
eager to shine
despite my black center

If you are a missing piece
I shall be a crescent moon
delighting in my deficiency

If you are distance
I shall be a lost traveller
never arriving my destination

If you are misery
I shall be clinically depressed
moping and crying all day

If you are death
I shall be terminally ill
kissing and embracing the Grim Reaper
counting down the days

Jackie Chou

Eternal Love

My love is rock solid
It is firmly grounded on earth

The Sun may vanish behind the clouds
The Moon may not rise one night

The mountains may move
And, rivers may run dry

Flowers may wither
And, colours may fade

My love for you is eternal
It can never, never die

My love is as pure as gold
And, as selfless as a tree

It is not lust that drives me
But, sheer innocence of my love

Lust may be momentary
But, true love is forever

Vincent Van Ross

Exhale

Where are you?

I don't know how much longer I can hold on?
Minutes turned to hours,
days turned to weeks,
weeks turned to months

Years, having now passed

How long must I wait?
How long must I live without you?
Tell me now,

So I can breathe again

Paige Turner

Betel Leaves

With eastern emerald splashes
And radiant half batting lashes
She whispered, her innermost, needs
Like vines bent her ankles and knees.

And much like them tasty betel leaves
She folded in and around me, tucked me
Into her opium-mouth, tucked me
Inside a secret sacred part of, herself.

"Our eternity has no windows - she said:
Whatever direction you take yourself,
Be sure your heart has partaken and dined
And, your soul is well fed".

Then placing an emerald leaf around my head
She embalmed me with a silken thread:
"Our eternity has no windows - she said:
But we too are butterflies jointly cocooned in a web"

Mark Andrew Heathcote

About Love

Two eyes;
one of sea and sky,
the other leaf and stone;
light borne and adrift,
flutter through an indifferent world's
shadows.

Until, at last,
now into the other, they sink.

Submerging and uniting;
while flanking phantoms scoff
and turn away, dejected.

A return – a horizon,
that only they can see.
A path – a purpose,
from which nothing can distract.

Hugh Burke

Cupid's Arrow

Fusion / Fission

the smallest space
exists between
two pairs of lips
pressed

two halves
of an atom
smashed
together

spliced
to slice
the universe
in half

Steven T. Licardi

A Lesson about Love

My Love...
Surrendering all of me to you
Blood dancing, surging, flowing
My heart...
Broken, as I blaze straight into the Autumn sunset
Cheeks the color of crimson
My Sweet...
Drowning ourselves in admonition
Completely confined by the distance between us
My Lesson...
Never, ever settle for less
Mountains are just mountains

Lyne Beringer

Cupid's Arrow

Longing and Desire

She was the girl next door,
Who came over to play.
He did his best to ignore,
Sometimes he'd run away.

He always liked her smile,
In a way, they were friends.
She had such a unique style,
On her, he always depends.

Over the years they changed,
Leading to a certain attraction.
His thinking was rearranged,
She gave him quite a reaction.

One day, when in High School,
They grew close and kissed.
Sometimes he acted the fool,
But he just couldn't resist.

Some called it puppy love,
But hearts were set on fire.
Dreaming on the stars above,
With a longing and desire.

First loves can be amazing,
Such a wonderful endeavor.
When love begins blazing,
Sometimes it lasts forever.

James F. Cunningham

Evermore

Some things, I wish I didn't see.
Like space between, you and me.
Recall how close we used to be.
The little twig, became a tree.
We sat in shade, in times of glee.
I gave a ring, from bended knee.
We shared our love, for all to see.
Our boundless love, could know no measure.
Burning passion, became our pleasure.
A smile from you, is now a treasure.
Or sit beside you, in times of leisure.
Never was, much cause to fight.
We both agree that, that's all right.
The flame may not seem, to be as bright.
Though you are still, my heart's delight.
And I will love you ever more.

Valormore De Plume

Where I Want to Be

I want to be in your arms
Cuddled up like a blanket
Expressing ourselves through sensual sign language

I want to be far away in our dreams
Escape with me for eternity
Beyond the universe is where I want to be

Just as long as the air I breathe…
Here with you is where I want to be

Tammy S. Thomas

Cupid's Arrow

Our Own Kind of Fairytale

For so long I wished that our love would resemble the fairy tales of romance I grew up believing. I dreamed of a perfect love where I was the girl with felicitous feet you foraged many villages for. I wished your lips were the dance floor for the words of affirmation I longed to hear and that somehow your tongue would waltz away with my wretched heart. But glass slippers shatter, and happily-ever-after exists only in bound pages. I needn't seek refuge in the safety of a knight's armor for you have gifted me with the unbridled strength I never knew I needed.

You brawled alongside me as I slay the beasts within I never imagined could be defeated. You have shown me patience and compassion as I learned to navigate turbulent waters through the guidance of your competent hands. Our story is no whimsical account of royal crusades of the heart; rather it is the tale of tainted lovers who helped to heal each other through courage, faith and understanding. And with each page composed of the ink spilled from our overflowing hearts I will love you more.

Dena M. Daigle

Written In the Stars

They say for each person
There is a certain Miracle from within
And you are meant to be just for one person
As time draws to a close to meeting the One,
The Universe and your Spirit Guides are on your side
To help you fulfil your One True Destiny.

It's written in the stars
And before you know it, I am coming to hold your hand
You may not know now but soon you'll get it somehow
I may have bumped into you along life's journey,
But you were too preoccupied with your own story
That you didn't notice me passing you by.

If in this life, we have to say goodbye
As my soul reincarnates, I'll meet you again in the next,
When our eyes lock as we cross our paths once more
You will know in your heart that it was me – your Destiny,
Just look at the stars on a beautiful night such as this
And know that the time is near to feel eternal bliss.

It's written in the stars
For even when True Love is lost,
Your soul will bleed for a meaning in your life
But though the inevitable happens, searching for your One True Destiny remains
If we are yet to discover our One True Miracle,
Even time may defeat itself in order for you to see me in another lifetime.

Elizabeth Esguerra Castillo

Cupid's Arrow

Love of My Life

Cupid's Arrow

Intimate Moments

Leveled plains of respect and love
Offer us to step outside of our self-concern.
Vulnerability is not a display of weakness but a
Extension of courage to meet in intimacy.

When I stand in front of you,
I am granted permission to just be me.
Life meeting life through two human hearts.
Life recognizing itself, and the effect is a joyous reunion.

No reference to time because we aren't going anywhere.
Our time is timeless.
The result of two people dwelling together in their hearts.

Learning to allow the healing potential
Existing within my human heart.
Touching you with tenderness

Understanding our "togetherness."
Sharing Human warmth.

Resulting in infinite patience and freedom
Expectations and judgments give wind,
Sexual desires released …
Taking us to the threshold of love.

Love will not let us rest.

Raja Williams

First published in The Journey Along The Way

An Eternal Reward

Is it only a dream
Distilled, in the broiling hearts of fools
Drunk and strung out
On the short-lived fumes?

Love
Is declared far and wide
Then lost between intervals of flying,
When tethered to the ground

To be coiled in its wrath
Through a lightning flash
Is an eternal reward

William Wright, Jr.

Paperback Writers

There is no dedication needed
It's not us we need to please
Everything now written
Ink to paper with such ease
I know you still remember
A time not long ago
I was your favorite all time lover
You were my mid-life handsome beau
We kept turning out the pages
Until we reached each chapter's end
Exhausting all our energy
Rehearsing every line again
When we finally found an ending
I stopped to take another look
Much to my amazement
We had completed our own book
There is such beauty in our writing
Replacing all the things we lack
We've sold a million copies
It's on the shelf in paperback

Lyne Beringer

Cupid's Arrow

I Cannot Say You are Perfect

What is it about the word,
perfect?
A still, cloudless day
The light projected through a window
A sky covered by stars
We keep these like jewels in our minds,
Their unbroken symphonies ringing
As fast as a wildfire through a forest
A key to the word which slips
From the mouth and crowns the receiver
It is a throne,
A sharp reward
But is perfect really what we love?
Because who has ever adored
A sky without its oddities
Spontaneous color swirling in a sunset
Is what intrigues anyone the most
What makes the light beautiful
Is the shadow which allows us
To see it in its contrast
And, love, what about the stars?
Would anyone ever watch
If they lined up in infinite chains
Across the sky?
It is the handfuls of lights
Flung across a black void
From which we find undefined brilliance
So, no

Cupid's Arrow

I cannot say you are perfect
I will not put you in so low
Of a pedestal
Because your eyes,
They are wondrous
Not for their *perfection*,
But for their unexpected moments
When you laugh
And they light up
Or when the sun shines
And they look like
Swirling pots of honey
My love for you
Finds itself within the
Beautiful grooves of
Your imperfect being
Because, after all,
The light seen from the world
Will always be slipping from the cracks
Flowers will only grow
If there is first rain
No memorable story has
Ever been without a bit of conflict,
And yours is far from over

Estelle Powell

Forgotten Places

Please kiss me in forgotten places, & always without haste,
Within the pleat of soft curving, around my dipping waist,
Please kiss me in that cave, deep behind my bended knee,
And within your special kisses, you'll always belong to me.

Please kiss me in forgotten places, but never ask me why,
Within the arching of my brow, & caressing my closed eye,
Please kiss me upon my tender lobe, of my ever heeding ear,
And deep within your dreams, my voice you'll always hear.

Please kiss me in forgotten places, of every form & shape,
Within the hollow of my throat, & the curl upon my nape,
Please kiss me, not only on my lip, breast, or on my cheek,
And by kissing my forgotten places, in passion, I'll be weak.

Sue Lobo

Be My Life

Be my life
Be my love
Take my hand
Embrace my being
Be though mine
Till time begins
And there remains no end
For in living
Death cannot quench
A love endured through
Calamities unbeknown
Come what may
Free my pain
Guide me forth
With bursting joy
Be my life
Be my love
Lead me to where nothing can compare
Kiss me gently
Touch my soul
Love me passionately
Without majesty
Be my life
Be my love
Make me
Your very own

Sylvana Accom

The Soul of Eternal Love

Chase me like a mirror
Into the silvery pond
Chase me like a bird
Into the buds of spring
Chase me like a flame
Along a candle wick
And there we'll share
The light of love
The birth of love.

Mark Andrew Heathcote

To: Two Doves

Ink your memory on canvas
Daydream of your blush melanin skin
I could drink from your lips
Night owl at your poinsettia
Never to forsaken;

Could one be so besiege by the first
Desire a second
And still be wholesome?

Could one be proportional devoted
To the butterfly
And the bee?

Among the rubbles of treasures
Envied was among Gold; Tanzanite
Within the wilderness
Lullaby you became
Never to be forsaken

Christena AV Williams

Cupid's Arrow

A Bee to a Flower

Your beauty is mesmerising
Your scent is intoxicating
Our meeting perhaps is predestined!
The world calls our relationship
A mere symbiosis but I call it
Another 'Romeo and Juliet'!
We both kiss each other so passionately
Perhaps that's the only way
I can shower my warmth
Upon your delicate radiant petals
And your floral nectaries
Where we marry each other.
I impregnate you with my amber body
We hug and our souls unite forever.
The fruit thus formed
Is an epitome of our immortal devotion.
I can see our demise
In our heated scarlet intimacy
The honey I make
Is a souvenir of your allure!

Sravani Singampalli

Cupid's Arrow

Closer View

I look through shards of glass for you
They cloud my memory and what is true
Distant shadows have faded you out
But I cast my hook and bait
Trying to resurface the vision of you
An outline in the fog, I thought I knew
Drawing closer, you try to reveal
A snapshot view that I can steal
My longing quest is drawing near
Because you have been lost, my dear
But I scour my steps to retrace
For you I could never replace
I clear my dusky slumbered mind
To capture what's lost, try to find
Our canvas to be painted new
A fresh start from my mind I drew
Finally I step through to your side
Without any reservations or pride
I'll soar to be in your life
I'll never give you any grief
Just pour your love into me
And I'll flood you with my sea
Your precious heart, mine to keep
Now my love, we'll deeply sleep
And wake with happiness in our hearts
Now replaced the puzzle parts
The four sides of our box complete
Take the past and hit delete

Michele Rice

Three Stanzas for My Beloved

1.

The bedcovers have recorded memories
Of us together in their very folds;
As the years roll, they will record
Many more, and the new ones, too,
Will have ever-fresh imprints of us.

2.

The scent of your perfume is on the pillows…
Now, all the pillows, old and new,
Are fragrant like you, and have your essence –
Colorful and bold.

3.

Love of my life, my beloved, every moment
I spend with you, is a gorgeous jewel
That never grows old, but remains forever
A magic dew on a sunlit morning –
Always young and new.

Jagari Mukherjee

I Remember

I remember
flipping through the pages
of other people's love stories

envisioning what mine
might look like someday

I remember
reading about the happily ever after
feeling jealous of the
flawless lovers
and the perfect endings

but, then,
I remember watching my parents
and their marriage
which brought more "for worse"
than "for better"

dad was sick
and mom was a nurse,
devoted to caring for him

I remember
stress and stretchers
waiting rooms and wailing ambulances
rushed but real kisses
given between nervous glances
and shaking hands
before doctors would whisk
him into the operating room

I remember watching her

Cupid's Arrow

always steady
and graceful
always prepared
and vigilant
in spite of the fear
I knew she felt

I remember each time
he would come home
she was waiting
to care for him
and give every ounce of her energy
to the wellbeing of the man she married

I remember
flipping through the pages
of fairytale love stories
and thinking,
"this isn't love.
this doesn't even begin to describe it."

And, I remember the realization
that the real love has always been
all around me

in a love
persisting through illness.
in the caring and comforting words
whispered over morning coffee
in the hands holding tight
in the back of the ambulance

in the eyes that have seen

Cupid's Arrow

so much pain,
but have persisted on
with the courage to keep loving

As I slammed the book closed,
I remember
witnessing the moments
of another couple's love story

praying that someday
I might find a love
that is so much more
than fair weathered fairy tales

That I might find a love
that keeps its promises
and bravely goes out into the unknown
feeling certain that
no circumstance can change it.

A love
Like the love of my parents.

Liz Newman

Cupid's Arrow

Caressing Clichés into Comforting Sighs

Mona and Scott
sitting in an oak tree
L-O-V-I-N-G
every acorn
that ruptures its seed
into aspects
of new beginnings
in a
L-I-F-E-T-I-M-E
of experiences
so full of bliss
they're sure to set
the world below
ablaze

Mona and Scott
sitting in an oak tree
K-I-S-S-I-N-G
the flames
that leap
ever higher
on fiery wings
of a
P-H-O-E-N-I-X
rising above
all the suffering
as a chemical combustion
ignites
in happiness
together

Scott Thomas Outlar

Cupid's Arrow

Take Me Away

Take me away
where there are no men
but birds and fish
heaven and earth
where there are no barriers
nor fences
where secrets are not secret
where you can shout your love
to the wind
away from prying eyes and
malicious whispers
from those who know nothing
of our inner worlds
and can't understand love
because never lived it

Take me away
to feel the thrill of being together
(surrender to passion)
where you can kiss my eyes, my lips
in the sunlight
and slowly make your hands slide
on my naked body

Take me away
to tell each other
what we kept silent
fill the time of innocent silences
caressed by the wind
loved by God

Maria Miraglia

Love Will Tear Us Apart

Missing

Like hearts caged deep within
One can neither glimpse nor hold
If a beat is lost, so shall be the rhythm
Before long, one falls into the cold

I'm caged when a part of me missing
Leaving behind the remaining shattered
Breathing nevertheless not living
Longing for the time they were gathered

Walking into heaven or falling down to earth
As each pace engraved its distinctive worth
If only it'd pound in its perfect rhythm
While you get to breathe & I'd be there to listen

Mahinour Tawfik

Cupid's Arrow

Another Scar

An eternal path of sunshine
until boredom strikes
Same shit every day,
nothing happens, do they?
I wonder, does even
'one' relationship last
when the sparkle is gone,
drowning in daily habits
These allegations it's being
all my fault, I turned into
such a tiresome person
Not up to something new,
something exciting
Obviously, the real me
is 'wearing'
In the beginning, when
you said you loved me,
it meant something
Now, I don't believe
you anymore
They are just hollow
empty words, I think
the love and fire between us
slowly starts to fade until
the flame will be extinguished
Same story from the past,
every time I really give myself
it always seems to end this way

Just want you to know,
I gave you everything I got
Tried to support you, to comfort you
and, that is my major mistake,

Cupid's Arrow

I let you take advantage of me
Caring and stupid me
At long last, I probably
end up all alone
I left everything behind
For you, just for you
Do you hear!
I don't know where this
leads to right now,
but I know you inflicted
another scar on my heart

Daginne Aignend

Bereft

I lived for the solitude,
For the quiet at three in the morning,
For the calm at midnight,
For the peace near a noisy fountain,
For the company at a lonely garden.
I lived when you left;
And if you come back,
Darling! It will be too crowded.
Let me embrace the melancholy
For I live when I am free,
For I am free when I am me,
Left alone but not lonely.
Oh! Don't come back!
This wait is happiness,
This grief is bliss,
Sleepless nights console,
Monotonic mornings comfort,
Living in memories, I am not.
I live in the space
Between the two worlds you left
Where you departed
And where we first met,
Where dreams were lived
Yet I was bereft...

Sanhita Baruah

Happiness in a Jar

You know she'll give you everything
You think you'll want or need
Stay forever trapped in loneliness
Just waiting to be freed
Questions race around her head
Afraid of answers she might find
Still she'll battle every monster
Locked away inside your mind
She wants nothing more than happiness
And yet her heart still aches
But she'll hold you in the darkness
Forgiving all of your mistakes
I wonder if you realize
Every sacrifice she's made
While waiting for the promises
That are constantly delayed
Blink and you might miss it
The fire dying in her eyes
Those baby blues are dripping wet
For all she's had to compromise
In the early morning hours
She makes a wish without a star

Happy just outside her reach
On a shelf inside a jar

Lyne Beringer

Cupid's Arrow

Rose Petals at My Feet

Rose petals at my feet look destitute
They're strewn all around my front garden path
They swirl like clouds trying to reconstitute
It pangs my heart that in their aftermath
Once again this summer draws to an end.
And my own, "Damask Rose", I gave my heart
Didn't open, wasn't for a minute my friend.
Rose petals at my feet will now depart
& winter shall arrive with snow & sleet
Spring & summer will come, never again.
Love deprived I shouldn't settle for conceit
Remembering a once, glowing, warm gem.
Rose petals at my feet foretell our end
No longer in this rose can I pretend?

Mark Andrew Heathcote

Resonance of Love

Patterned pain from the lost kindred
resonance of love felt by the heartless
wanton telling of tales in lost tongue
a whistling rhyme vibrates in an ear.
Tasting dreams of all spoiled children
orbs adrift disappearing before dawn
a pious discontent is left in the soul
liars are rigid cowering underground.
Alight upon the head of an icy needle
street urchins smile for a lone dollar
a red tide abates at the lowest ebb
whirling about we simply wait to die.
Unrequited causation in a feted toddy
watch lava destroy all lonely memoirs.
Scribe your lines to this winter's crush
the resonance of love now drifting away.

Ken Allan Dronsfield

Cold Moon

Forever remained the roses after you left,
Though locked away in the cupboard of memory…
The moon wore a wintry look.

And the cold moon
Took the place of my heart
Which yet cherished
The dried roses.

Something deep hurts
In the cold-moon heart
Because I never dreamt
That Love will tear us apart.

Jagari Mukherjee

Saved by Words

Convinced I would be
forever imprisoned
in our marriage, I couldn't
find a backdoor, a way out
The only escape was the
dream world of social media
Blandished by fake compliments,
soothed by meaningless statements,
made me realize, I never
have felt so alone before
Struck by oppressive desperation,
created the inevitable urge
to write about my dejected feelings
A poem was born ...
My cry of distress gave
an unforeseen response
Cupid fired a written arrow
through our longing hearts
Saved by words

Daginne Aignend

Cupid's Arrow

Tale of Woe

My heart is weighed down and I can't tell
For you won't comprehend and I don't know
How much misery - in a heart can dwell
Dare not look deep, there are tales of woe

Ahead of titles, engraved "Farewell"
Every smile sows seeds of throes
Jaded with wondering if it's heaven or hell
So here's my heart, darling - I bestow

Will you hold it tight or let it hail?
After you have become another tale?

Mahinour Tawfik

The Bubble Bursts

Sugar-coated
jelly bean words
transforms into
acid etched venom
Pink clouds whispers,
changes in an outburst
of viscous bitterness
Like a
sweet-scented Syringa
suddenly starts to spread
a stinking stench
Brutally awoken out
of my airy-fairy dreams
I wish I had
never met
You

Daginne Aignend

Cupid's Arrow

Love vs. Lust

Drifting With the Clouds

Closing my eyes,
I visualize us on a blanket in the middle of the meadow
Two souls as one, intertwined in the essence of the moment
Time stands still, the clouds drift by
Holding on to one another, lost in love
Sharing the pleasures of the flesh
Uniting our souls with the energy of the Universe
Love explodes as we let go
Basking in the afterglow
Drifting along with the clouds

Jill N. Pontiere

Living in Loves Illusion

We claimed to love one another
But we were not truthful about our love
Our feelings based on sexual desires
And the meeting of our needs

We found escape in our loving moments
Filling our own, internal voids
Living in loves illusion
Something we tried so hard to avoid

Wanting to hold you close to me
To fill my desires needs
But our lack of true depth
Brings out jealousy

You break into a million pieces
Expectations left unfulfilled
When you're filled with envy
I cannot be your shield

Because I know the difference
Possessiveness and jealousy
Have no room in love
I hold you one last time

And I let you go in love.

Raja Williams

First published in Imprints In The Sand

I Am One With You

I am one with you
You fill each crevasse deep inside me
Like the waves turn
You wave me into ecstasy
I feel your breath so deep within in my soul
To touch you
To feel you
I wrap myself around you
You are my night
Within each day
You ride me into glory
Hold me tight
Don't ever let go
For in letting go
You take my soul
An leave an empty shell behind
Without you
No me can be found
Embrace me lovingly
Love me passionately
Take me gently
My heart aches for you
With an unquenchable thirst
You quake inside me
Bursting forth with insurmountable joy
I am one with you
You are my end
You are my alpha
You are my long-awaited soul-mate

Sylvana Accom

Moonlight Away

Let me take you on a walk
To the moon tonight, Beloved.
The words of your lips
Are like grapes
Fresh from the vine.

Your smile has in it the miracle
Of turning water into wine.

Let me adorn you
With the finest robes.

Your name is like fragrant resin
In a choice ointment.

I see a river of oil
Flow from your lips, my darling.

The rainbow I see in your eyes
Expands the borders of my dream.

The rainbow I see is the rainbow
In your eyes.

Your love is the fragrance,
And my heart the flower of new Eden.

Shola Balogun

Cupid's Arrow

Looks

He looked at me with hunger in his eyes
as if I were his prey; something he had stalked

When I looked into his eyes
I knew he wanted to devour me; tasting every inch of me

I liked the way he looked at me

Paige Turner

Cupid's Arrow

The Day I Wake To Find You

The day I wake to find you beside my naked self
Your arm's warm embrace engulfing my spirit
Your hands dead on its weight enclosing my breast
Your morning breath, heavenly fanning my face
And your eyes slowly open to find me staring
Sweet smile slowly forms both our lips
Knowing we're each other's first sight of a beautiful morn

Memories filled my mind
With our night full of love
Remembering how beautiful it was
Skin to skin joined together as one
Each sigh, each touch, each kiss...
Felt so good, so right, so at home.

For with you, at last, I found
That pull, that magic that others had
Heart-melting lava of wet insides
Longing for a throb only from your burning rod
Just like a sonnet with syllables in count
We form a world rhyming the both of us

I welcome you with legs apart
Your member so rigid, so silky and wanting
Our pores open, slippery, burning
Each contact, electrifying, satisfying
Each taste, passionately sweet, addicting
As we come to our peak, a new height starts to rise.

Starry night, cold, heat, spring rain
Everything happening all at once
Passion filled our heart with higher calling that is love
Exhausted, fulfilled, aware of what this was

Cupid's Arrow

As we close our eyes, our spirit soar
Knowing that tomorrow, each will still be there

Your heartbeat speaks to me as I drifted to sleep
Mine singing a sonata that only you could hear
As consciousness slowly shut down
A dim light remains at the corner
Keeping us together, even in our dreams.

We float in darkness, swimming in each other's warmth
Knowing that a new dawn would come and there would still be us
The day I wake to find you beside me, with me, forever.

Gigi Lee

Perspiration

It's the nectar of your body that I love, & nightly smell,
The film of saline gloss, where your belly starts to swell,
It's the drop of beaded dew, upon your downy upper lip,
Those runnels upon your skin, that drip below your hip.

It's the oasis where your armpit, embraces rounded breast,
Ripples of sweet elixir, that lets no man sleep, nor ever rest,
That mustiness of living, slaking tired soul & errant tongue,
Whence from bed sheet & body, every droplet's duly wrung.

It's the moisture of our loving, cracking drought's hard shell,
Rivulets slow-snaking, into inner thigh's soft & deepest well,
The sweat upon your brow, & behind your bent rounded knee,
The perspiration from your pores, is my slicked & salted sea.

Sue Lobo

Summer, Ocean

When the quake thundered
it was you beneath me
breaking apart
against
the sweat of skin
the raw sea
flushed from your body
the in and out tides

It was you who broke
like waves
bringing me to the scent
to the warm liquid of your thighs
to the leather hardness
of my charge

You, the matador
drinking the bull's blood
Me, the bull
goring you into ecstasy
until we lay finished off
our trembling bodies
smelling of ocean summers

Dah

The Goddess of Love

With sky now framing our quantum desire
Of us mindful mortals, you, love's Goddess require.
Eros is awakened, and expansive in scope, -
Absolute abandon, with excitement in hope.
Expressly so purposed, demonstrative in love;
Endorsed by the angels of yon, and above.
Exquisitely chiselled, and enamoured to toe,
You're marked by my arrow so sprung from my bow.
Now postured by habit, as reluctant to wake,
Do make of this moment an advantage to take;
Warmed in the pleasure with libido awake,
With perfumed insistence, we lovers must mate.

Audley Hitchins

The Millennials

We are a generation of cynics.
We are a generation of instant coffee and quickies in parking lots.
But we weren't born this way.
We were kids who believed;
Believed in superheroes and fairy tales.
Believed in a love that lasts over a thousand eternities.
In our books love conquered all and good triumphed over evil.
But then we were forced to grow up.
Get real and run a race of which no one is coming out alive.
We fought, lost, betrayed and cheated.
We ran over the things that may have saved us.
You know the hole we feel all the time in our chest?
The one we are unable to fill no matter what we do.
We all got that and only a few of us will be lucky enough to fill that.
Love can fill that hole - the eternal kind.
The kind we stopped believing in
the last time someone broke us.
You may think I'm naive, even stupid maybe.
But I found it - I found my eternity in her.
And I was stupid enough to let it go.
But if I get a chance to hold her over everything I have, I'll take it in a heartbeat.
You know why?
Because only the times she held me, I felt whole again.

Sagar Singh

Love is Forever

A Velvet Dawn

As blustery winds bring winter snows ...
I wait for you by the old cart path.
the full moon hides as I wish you love ...
This love from me to you.
I feel it strong through the velvet dawn ...
as I wait for your return.
A barren stare through a mirrors glare ...
I know that you are there.
A serene promise and blessings to share ...
I sit and love only you.
The season's may change, trees now bare...
I'll miss you and forever will care.
My heart waits only for you.

Ken Allan Dronsfield

Someday

Someday we will sit again
Where we so lovingly used to do.
We will talk of all that's been
And all that we missed too.

We'll look into each other's eyes,
We'll get back all that we need.
We'll sit and smile and see
Love, eventually succeed.

The wonderful evening
Will bring a beautiful night.
Love we will cherish
When we reunite.

And so someday I'll laugh off
All the years I stayed maroon.
But all I can hope for now
Is that someday comes soon.

Sanhita Baruah

Cupid's Arrow

The Soul of My Life

In the midst of lofty mountains
You seek out a mountain pass

In the inky blue sky of night
You travel like a shooting star

On jagged, rocky terrain
You flow playfully like a river

On the dry, parched land
You descend like the rain

When the ocean is in turmoil
You arrive like a rescue boat

When there is flash flood
You turn into an island

You hold the key to the child's toy
That makes it come alive

You are the force that drives me
You are the soul of my life

Vincent Van Ross

In the Delta

You are ocean.
I am river.
You sing to me
In waves of three.
"Run to me. Run
To me. Run to
Me."

Our night-lit longing turns to vapor in the sun.
Lonely sighs are clouds.
You send rain to fill my springs,
Engorging me. In rapids rush,
I will, to meet you
In the delta.

In the delta,
In the delta,
I will bring you perfumed flowers from the mountain
When I run into your arms
In the delta.

In the delta,
In the delta
You will welcome me with salty kisses
And we'll dance our undulating waltzes
In the delta.

In the delta,
In the delta

Cupid's Arrow

I will bring my fresh rain water back to you
That you can sing, again, to me in waves of three.
"Run to me. Run
To me. Run to
Me."

Sandra Lyon Kramer

A Rare Luminosity

Smiles rise like sudden suns
when I think about her.
She is new, fresh, not like the others.
These thoughts spark a euphony
within my veins that burst
like orchids in simultaneous bloom.
I've found a rare brightness
from out the droves of darkness,
a luminosity that can be kindled,
night or day, with the mere thought
of her. My heart palpitates as her
personality pours forth a percussion of light,
a dance of rich colors suddenly aflutter,
as her words intrigue. The depth
of her discourse illuminates, perplexes
and vexes my mind. Yes! I have found
a rare light. The excitement of what
she'll say next pulses through my veins,
so grateful to have found such an incandescence
among this dull and darkly world.

Heath Brougher

First Kissed

I look in your eyes
To remember the sun
And those days
We played on the ground
I hear your pure voice
To remember your song
And those days
So blessed with the sound
I smell your cool breath
To remember the rain
And the days
We walked in the mist
I touch your wet lips
To remember the stars
And those days
Sweet times we first kissed

John Walker

Forever Love

Love reaches past
life and death

connecting two souls,
hearts entwined
in an immortal embrace

holding tightly
transcending all obstacles
and always finding a way
back to each other

it's the only thing
that can make us feel
so alive and so afraid
all at once

it is immensity,
overflowing life with clarity.
It changes you
from the inside out

from the day you fall,
your whole life will change
from the day you let it in,
you'll never be the same

Liz Newman

Happy Mother's Day

Had I my life to live again,
All that I know is this:
Passion would still find me when,
Perchance, your lips I'd kiss;
Your love has been pure bliss.

Many times I've thought about
Our life, and how it's been
Togetherness year in and out,
Heartfelt love 'til the end;
Every time we did without
Restored our faith, my friend,
Since our love always mends.

Dearest one, just let me tell you,
All my love is yours,
Yes, today and toujours.

John Lambremont, Sr.

Our Story

The gaze
We hold
Tells the story
Of our world
The whispers
We exchange
Tells the story
Of our years
The dreams we combine
Tells the story
Of our hopes
The depths
We survive
Tells the story
Of our tears

John Walker

Anniversary

Another year we've been together;
Never have I loved you more;
Newlyweds at heart forever
In all climes and on all shores;
Verses I shall write you ever;
Ever to you I implore:
Raise my life up, make me better,
So much better than before;
Always my love exceeds letters,
Reaching new heights as it soars;
You, my love, I do adore.

John Lambremont, Sr.

Cupid's Arrow

Love Changes Everything

I.V.

Love
is a slow-drip.

Vinyl bag of saline certainty.
A taste that fills your veins
and corrupts your brain

or maybe
that's just me.

Sure,
the hot and heavy nuclear winter
that follows atomic ecstasy
is a wonderful way to claim
a new
eviscerated
reality,

but I prefer
a slow-burn.

A strangeness that creeps.

Nearly excruciating,
the sense that something has changed
about a room we furnish alone.
Atriums
locked from within,
without reflective surfaces.

You know,
the way keys look like mountains
you'll never climb?

Cupid's Arrow

Yeah, me neither.

But the thought that you and I might
and the knowledge that we will
fills the cracks,
nooks, bumps.

Man, that's the rub.

When skin once touched
transforms,
unfurls
beneath our thumbs.

The hum that reverberates
through pain
to remind you that you
are not
the only one.

I prefer to putz,
clumsy and fussy,
through the shadows of love.

The changing colors of walls.
So subtle, so slow,
you almost
do not notice.

Almost.

Steven T. Licardi

Lucky in Love

The world
is mad winds and rains
and you are my shield

plucking me
from the cracks
where I lived
like a wildflower

you hold me
like a precious jewel
the dust and dirt
brushed away
with your touch

Now I waltz around
thinking every love song
is about us

words of my heart
show on my blushed cheeks
for the world to see

Jackie Chou

Meeting

You spoke to me.

A smile on your lips
and a sadness
behind your eyes
to match my own.
I could see it,
recognise it.
I knew it well.

"Hello you", I said.
"Hello me?"

A gesture,
a question in your voice,
laughter caught
in the back of your throat
and eyes that smiled.
Momentarily.

At least
momentarily
understanding.

Lynn White

Cupid's Arrow

My Stranger

I was pleased to be just me
Unaffected, jolly and sometimes, serene
Other times angry, but otherwise happy
Then you came and everything changed
I felt a sudden missing that wasn't there before
I don't want nor need it, but loneliness persisted
In my heart, something constantly grows so painfully
A hallow within, aching to be filled by something

I looked the other way, walking past by you
Convinced myself that only if I faithfully ignore
Would the malady be gone and I would be cured
Much like a bad wind gushing fleetingly ahead
I am fine, I could take it if I could just hold it in
I closed my eyes and run blindly away
The further I am, the less affected I'd be
I'll be happy alone, just like before...

Or so I thought, but I was wrong
The more I denied, the more it pains
The more I run away, the more tired I became
I could never be free, distance is just an illusion
What I really needed, is to be with you
No one else would fit this empty hollow
Without you, a half-life is what I would follow
Like a moon without the sun on its horizon

So won't you, take me with you?
Would you love me as I do?
Forgive my foolishness and embrace me instead

Cupid's Arrow

With your eyes in tears and a smile on your face.
Will you accept my heart, broken as it is?
Of my own doing and no one else
Please fill me in and make me whole

Gigi Lee

Baggage

I dragged it with me . . .
every
    hurt,
        rejection,
            strain,
and every other fragile moment of disappointment

All of my past heartbreaks brought . . .
fear,
    disappointment,
        pain,
            anxiety,
and all the unhappy endings that go with failed relationship's.

For years I buried all those feelings in . . .
deep,
    quiet,
        forgotten,
            places
where I learned to forget the feelings and emotions related to heartbreak.

Then suddenly one day you came along . . .
and
    my
        baggage
            is
                wide
                    OPEN.

Raja Williams

Fall in Love

Come, fall in love
When the sky's so bright,
See me, hold me
When there's still light,
May be darkness
Will take away this life,
Turn it into
A dream of the night...

Come, rise in love
When the birds fly so high,
Take me with you
To the mountains not nigh,
May be summer
Will melt all the ice,
Flood our love
With the river of spite.

Come, fall in love
With the song I sing,
Make me wear
Your love's ring,
May be a storm
Will come, deafening,
Take away my love
And the songs I'm singing.

Come, rise in love
With the trees that play,
And we'll too
Dance the day away,
May be rain
Will spoil this day,

Cupid's Arrow

Falling trees
And us, locked away.

Come, fall in love
When the day's fine,
We are together
Like a tale divine,
May be forever
Is an illusion, a lie.
Cherish today.
Rest fate did destine.

Sanhita Baruah

Cupid's Arrow

Make Love to Me

Please tantalize me, with those ancient lost tales,
I ask only that you pleasure me, with poetry scribed,
Tease me with quatrains, & tickle me with trilogies,
And caress me with softly, with cantatas of whales.

Kiss me, with the urgent kindling of ritual's old fires,
Love me longingly & languidly, with lace-clad lyrics,
Adore me, with the chanting of wise hooded Druids,
And play me please, upon strings of harps & old lyres.

Sing me songs of long ago, & those of way back when,
Meld me with melodies, from nightingale's gold nebs,
Pray me within God's prayers, of adoration & homage,
And please make love to me, in ways unknown to all men.

Sue Lobo

Petals

Sepals fall off softly, one at a time, floating to the ground
Underneath like silk, a satin welcome
Exposed
Now sun kissed and laid bare; feel the breath of Spring on your stem

The breath of new Spring, connect with the seed
Exposing the rose button
Within this opening; feel the breath of Spring on your stem
So close, the flowering petals

Exposing the rose button
Inflorescence
So close, the flowering petals
Spring's mounting ascent

Efflorescence
Exposed
Spring's breathless release
Sepals fall off softly, one at a time, floating to the ground

Linda Imbler

Dormant

You cannot capture the potential of a person to love
in the span of a single kiss.

Such hypotheses are inherently lethal,
because a kiss is a contaminated sample.

One part you. One part me.
Two parts infinite.
Infinity squared -
Two souls raised to the highest power.

There exists no formula for the formulation of love.

I know... I've tried.

Bashed my head against the incubation chamber,
because love is a stillborn child when its
premature birth does not allow room for it to breathe.

Please.

Have patience with me.

My lungs have not yet formed the capacity
to grow themselves into bellows, to blow the smolder
of former spontaneous combustion back into a blaze.

Yet, I yearn to hold my skin to the flames,
to press the napalm to my lips,
to know its warm is safe enough
to bask in.

Cupid's Arrow

Body heat is the only thing
that separates a poet from a page,
although you may find yourself
immortalized
in one or the other.

I wonder…

What do you suppose bears dream about
when they're hibernating?

I have a theory:
They dream
about being
bears.

But I think,
in many ways...

Love?

Love does he same thing.

Steven T. Licard

Dialect

Love stirs two souls into speaking
their own invented dialect

It parts lips
flexes lungs
shapes the breath into sounds only they
understand

Restrained embraces
uncertain kisses
translate themselves into a voice

Listen…one is whispering:
"I need you closer."

Like only across bridges, desolate nights
comprehend the freight train's desperate
wail.

Like only the plummeting hawk must feel –
careening back into flight at the searing
call of its mate.

Like only a cello's mournful sigh can
beckon the piano to nestle against it,
softening.

They hear one another, and respond.

Hugh Burke

Convergence

Can I make myself, as a gift to you?
Will you cherish that which I whisper
to your troubled mind, when night falls
and eyes are heavy from your burdens

Can I offer myself as a pyre of love?
Lay upon me, swaddled in my softness,
covering, converging, consuming
till your peace is found within me

Let me stroke your weary brow
smother you with feathered kisses
taste your skin upon my tongue
speak tender words into your heart

I'll be your gift
I'll be the pyre
I'll soothe your mind
I'll be the fire

Brenda-Lee Ranta

Cupid's Arrow

Love Never Dies

A Letter to My Soulmate

I am fully present in this moment, nestled comfortably in your arms.
I silently admire the melody composed by your heartbeat syncopating to match the rhythm of my own.
Electric impulses course through my veins with but a glimpse into your eyes.
I see the very future of my soul amidst two oceanic orbs and I humbly thank the universe for giving this fickle heart of mine a home.
Because of you, I have learned the true meaning of commitment and loyalty.
You have given me the strength to fly high above all the heights I have ever wished to reach.
While others have crumbled beneath the weight of my spirit, you never let my feet touch the ground.
Our destiny is forever connected by pulse, even surpassing the barriers of time and space.
If ever I doubted reincarnation, our love is the sweetest affirmation, and I promise to cherish you through all of this life and the next.

Dena M. Daigle

Joie de Vivre

Throughout the lonely nights the lady wept in pain
Memories of the time she spent with her soldier refused to wane
She lit a lamp every night with a prayer on her lips
Every hour at night she checked the flickering wick
Throughout the night she poured her heart's anguish
Through soulful notes on her sitar
She played with so much joie de vivre,
That God's above too shed golden tears
Every note sanctified her love for her soldier
The music united the lady with her distant lover
The clock on the wall had stopped, stalling time
Time and lady waited fervently for the door bell's chime
One morning the clock tick-tocked again
There was a rainbow in the sky with verdant rain
A tall sinewy figure was spotted walking down her lane
The doorbell chimed, the door flew open
There was no need for any words lame
All pain ebbed from the lady's slender frame
The sun shone again through her love-struck eyes
Fusing her lips with his she claimed her soul's prize.

Paromita Mukherjee Ojha

Cupid's Arrow

Tinge of Tears in the Mist

I'm leaning on the oak tree
Listening to our cherished song;
the lyrics run down my cheeks and
the melody hugs and tugs at my soul.
A time to breathe; a time to dream,
a time to wonder; or ponder the illusion;
while birds flutter about the leaves,
in this mist I feel you closer.
Tears in the autumn mist fall
by the winding chilly brook;
The memories beget a peace;
continuing down a winding path.
Follow me where the Sun
warms my fallen essence;
then softly whisper a sonnet
to serenade a dispirited heart.
Wipe these stinging tears
from my whetted cheek once more
I'll return at sunrise once again,
to embrace the memory that is you.

Ken Allan Dronsfield

Blue

Blue skies, blue sea,
a day of sparkling sunshine,
with a shimmering horizon.
And then, out of this blue,
You,
smiling sadly with your lovely blue eyes.

I knew you from the back, you said,
the cut of your hair, your bright blue mac.
I wanted to see your face again,
it's only fair, you've seen mine.
You must have done,
me, being who I am.

I wanted to smell your clean hair smell.
So I took a chance, and here I am.
I wanted to
abate the sadness.

I nodded. Yes.
I know it's true.
It's all been said
and we won't be sad.
No blue moods
on this bright blue day
of smiling sunshine.

We'll go together now,
for now
and be glad.
After all,
one way or another,
everything will end

Cupid's Arrow

in tears, I said,

So let's take our now time
and chance the rest.

Lynn White

Cupid's Arrow

Heaven's Last Wish

Celestial space, within its infinite realm,
the prayers so distinct, constant, not weakened nor turned aside,
the wish for clean links, for reconnection.

This satisfied, long sought gift one day will come,
heartache diminished, then once and for all wounds healed.

You went to your grave, your song not yet done.
Grim future partings, no longer hold us bound.
We, no longer hostage, the universe has listened.

We can tell each other words learned, from the sky song
or we'll sing to each other our own lyrics.

Love once deferred, once stayed by death's divide,
replaced, renewed, reflected.

We meet as once agreed, a promise made while living,
having wished true, and for time lost, be forgiving.

Linda Imbler

Cupid's Arrow

Love

One is born in the quest for love
But what's love but pain and woe
Painters and poets all speak of
Before the end, most drown below

Diamond stars in dreamy skies
Raindrops falling on cupid's arrows
Thunder falls and the angel dies
Ruby red the painting goes

On the balcony Juliet awaiting Romeo
To beat the kindred – grasp her heart
But through her blood, poisons flowed
Romeo flees before the battle starts

Mahinour Tawfik

Galveston

And you asked me
to walk along the sandy shores
in bare feet,
and I complained about the sand
burning my soles.
And if someday,
something happened to you,
I would walk on hot coals
to bring you back.

And you asked me
to get in the water,
and I complained
that I could not see the bottom.
And if someday
something happened to you,
I would endure jellyfish stings
to bring you back.

Now someday is here.
You asked for such small things.
How I wish I could re-answer the past!

Linda Imbler

Thinking about Ex-boyfriend

Photos of
the London Eye
Middlesex University
Happy family gatherings
smile on my friend's
Facebook Timeline

I like them
Then I change
the thumb up symbol
to a red heart –
a love symbol
that suits much more
my true affection

I close my eyes
Memories fly 15 years back
A rush at the post office
Birthday gifts
End of year gifts
were ready for the flight

Oh Pete!
I wonder where you are
Do you still remember me?
Do you still like
Emily Dickinson's poems?
What about D.H Lawrence?
What do you think
of Carol Ann Duffy's poetry?
Do you still talk of
psychology, philosophy and spirituality?

Cupid's Arrow

Pete, do you still teach IT
with much patience
to special needs students?
Do you still stay late evenings
and conduct counseling sessions?

Oh, where are you?
Do you still remember
our regular phone calls
and the romantic holiday plans?
Do you remember how conflicts
never existed between us?
Everything was summarized into
"I understand."

Oh, my dearest Pete!
You have been
my true love
the only man
who has understood
my sensitive heart
my intellectual needs
my inquisitive mind

Oh Peter!
I still dream of
your coming back
in my life.

Vatsala Radhakeesoon

Hold

Hold my hand
While spring blooms
During fall leaves

Hold my hand
In a crowd
On a deserted beach

Hold my hand
When I am laughing
While tears run down my cheeks

Hold my hand
Starting now
Until my last breath

Maggie Mae

Empty Pillow

I can
still smell
your scent
upon this
empty pillow
which you
vacated months
ago.

So, in
a way,
you never
left and
I still
hold you
close every
single night.

Heath Brougher

Counting Stars

Your light,
The beautiful brightness of smiling eyes
Now closed in sleep.
Perhaps I should not weep,
But I do.
I do love you.

I feel the absence of your light
Like a shadow on these unfamiliar paths
That I must walk without you.
But the brilliance of your spirit is infinite as stars.
I do not need to count them all to know they shine.
Like those million, billion suns,
Your light still moves in spaces here,
In me.

Ray of love and hope,
In darkness you are with me.
Always,
In me you are shining in your beauty.

In all these coming nights
When I look to heaven
I will see you.
I will count your sun as: "One."
The brightest,
Only one.

Sandra Lyon Kramer

Her Metaphor

The very essence of him
permeated her every sense;
seeped in her hidden shadows
he was as familiar as a lullaby
his voice soothing to her ears

He was the metaphor for
everything her heart recalled
of infinite love and union
long before their limbs entwined
she had always known his soul

She often shuttered in fear
When he still loved the world,
forgetting his soul had loved
her first, long before birthing
into the sphere of human trial

She sees glimpses of confused
recognition flicker within his
eyes, in his sideways glances
Lo, he is not yet fully awake;
his soul is still softly sleeping

So, she lets him rest
until he remembers;
there is time enough

until he remembers

Brenda-Lee Ranta

Cupid's Arrow

A Winter's Love (Later in Life)

I have weathered the seasons
My youth was filled with fields of blossoms
Was afraid to venture into to pastures to pollinate the flowers as they were starting to bloom
Would just peer over the fence from afar
I was shy and had no confidence
O but when summer came
Danced in the field and enjoyed the summer
Maybe a bit too much
Covered in pollen and loving it
Settled with one flower that caught my eye and planted seeds that grew
Didn't tend to them the way I should
Before I knew the coldness of winter had come
Had some pleasure in the autumn and fall but the happiness did not last
Decided to face it alone
Told that nothing grows in winter
Everything withers and dies
But that is no true
The sun still shines and brings warmth
And it in this time that I have discovered
There is Love even in winter

Nolan P. Holloway, Jr.

# Epilogue

Publishing Assistance

Starving Artist

In 2013 Ms. Raja Williams realized that there was a gap, a void if you will, within the publishing industry. A writer either had to come up with hundreds, sometimes thousands of dollars to release a book or take on the journey of self-publishing alone. There was no middle ground, no one there to assist, either financially or lead the way in self-publishing. Most writers do not have the finances to pay a publisher, and some don't know where to start when it comes to self-publishing, nor are they prepared to be in business for themselves.

Raja was inspired to start a fund to assist writers in becoming published authors at either a discounted rate or a full publishing scholarship. To begin this fund Raja paid for the publishing of our first anthology *Love, a Four Letter Word*, comprised of poets from all around the world. The sales generated from the purchases of the book were placed into a fund that enabled us to fund future publishings.

Cupid's Arrow

We now are able to offer anthology publications, a chance for authors to have a voice in the literary world yearly, and we have been able to offer several authors full scholarships, as well as offering deeply discounted publishing services as a whole. We are thankful for the continued support of this program by both our readers and writers alike.

For More Information Please Visit Our Website At:

www.ctupublishinggroup.com/starving-artist-fund.html

Cupid's Arrow

Creative Talents Unleashed

Get Connected With Us!

Website: Creative Talents Unleashed Publishing Group

www.ctupublishinggroup.com

Facebook: Get connected with us on our Facebook Page

www.Facebook.com/Creativetalentsunleashed

Twitter: https://twitter.com/CTUPublishing

Blog: www.creativetalentunleashed.com

Pinterest: https://www.pinterest.com/creativetalents/

Instagram: https://instagram.com/ctupublishinggroup/

About the Book

"Love." Such an exquisite word. It is the fundamental longing of every human soul. It can also be the undoing of the human heart. We may search for wealth, success, freedom, stature and prestige, but underneath it all, there is no lasting joy in any of that without that someone, that one special person that loves us, champions us as we champion them, and shares our every mistake and victory with us. "Love." That sometimes, illusive yearning we hold secretly inside, the need to be of importance to someone, the need to have someone who is important to us; the most basic, yet the most important human desire, is the pinnacle of our lives or the undoing of it.

This exquisite Anthology, a collection of sublime poems and prose, tells of the essence of love, as music to the ears and the stirring to our hearts. From "Love at First Sight," to "Love Never Dies," every facet of love is gloriously depicted in the many lovely chapters given to us from these gifted poets.

Come, fall in love, remember the taste of it, the feel of it within. Come cry a few tears, then rejoice its victories.

"Love." conquers all.

Brenda-Lee Ranta, author of *A Soul Passenger*

Creative Talents Unleashed

Creative Talents Unleashed is an independent publishing group that offers writers an opportunity to share their writing talents with the world. We are committed to fostering and honoring the work of writers of all cultures. Our publishing group offers writing tips to assist writers in continued growth and learning, daily writing prompts and challenges to keep the writers mind sharp and challenged, marketing and events, as well as a variety of yearly publishing opportunities. We are honored to be assisting writers in the journey of becoming published authors.

www.ctupublishinggroup.com

For More Information Contact:

Creativetalentsunleashed@aol.com

www.ingramcontent.com/pod-product-compliance
Lightning Source LLC
Chambersburg PA
CBHW061329040426
42444CB00011B/2832